PATRICIA KRISTOFFERSEN'S
Beautiful Borders
Baby Blankets ™

Rings for Baby
Page 6

Precious Moments
Page 2

...cious in Pink
...e 10

Buttercup
Page 14

His & Hers Garden
Page 18

Precious Moments

Skill Level
■■■■ EXPERIENCED

Finished Size
37 x 37 inches

Materials
• Red Heart Baby Econo medium (worsted) weight yarn (7 oz/675 yds/198g per skein):
  • 2 skeins #1570 lavender
  • 1 skein each #1680 pastel green, #1224 baby yellow, #802 baby blue, #1722 light pink
• Sizes G/6/4mm and H/8/5mm crochet hooks or size needed to obtain gauge
• Tapestry needle
• 4 plastic bags to hold skeins of yarns

Gauge
Size G hook: 5 dc = 1 inch

Pattern Notes
Weave in ends as work progresses.

Join rounds with a slip stitch unless otherwise stated.

Chain-3 at beginning of double crochet rounds counts as first double crochet unless otherwise stated.

Chain-4 at beginning of double crochet round counts as first double crochet and chain-1 space unless otherwise stated.

Special Stitches
Front post treble crochet cluster (fptr cl): Holding back last lp of each fptr on hook, 2 fptr around indicated st, yo, draw through all 3 lps on hook.

Beginning popcorn (beg pc): Ch 3, 3 dc in indicated sp, drop lp from hook, insert hook from front to back in 3rd ch of beg ch-3, draw dropped lp through st.

Popcorn (pc): 3 dc in indicated sp, drop lp from hook, insert hook from front to back in first dc of 3-dc group, draw dropped lp through st.

Beginning shell (beg shell): Ch 4, (dc, ch 1, dc) in indicated sp.

Shell: [Dc, ch 1] twice in indicated sp, dc in same sp.

Instructions

Block 1
Make 24.

Rnd 1: With size G hook and lavender, ch 4, join with sl st in first ch to form a ring, **ch 3** *(see Pattern Notes)*, 2 dc in ring, ch 2, [3 dc in ring, ch 2] 3 times, join in 3rd ch of beg ch-3. Fasten off. *(12 dc, 4 ch-2 sps)*  *purple*

Rnd 2: Join baby blue with sl st in any ch-2 sp, ch 3, (dc, ch 2, 2 dc) in same sp *(beg corner made)*, *dc in next dc, **fptr cl** *(see Special Stitches)* around next dc, dc in next dc, (2 dc, ch 2, 2 dc) in next ch-2 sp *(corner made)*, rep from * twice, dc in next dc, fptr cl around next dc, dc in next dc, join in 3rd ch of beg ch-3. Fasten off.

Rnd 3: Join pastel green with sl st in any corner ch-2 sp, **beg pc** *(see Special Stitches)* in same sp, *ch 2, dc in next 3 dc, holding back last lp of each st on hook, (dc, **fpdtr** *{see Stitch Guide}* around same dc on rnd 2 as last dc made, fpdtr around next dc on rnd 2, dc) in next fptr cl, yo, draw through all 6 lps on hook, working in back of last fpdtr, dc in next 3 dc, ch 2, **pc** *(see Special Stitches)* in next ch-2 sp, rep from * 3 times, ch 2, dc in next 3 sts, holding back last lp of each st, (dc, fpdtr around same dc on rnd 2 as last dc made, fpdtr around next dc on rnd 2, dc) in next fptr cl, yo, draw through all 5 lps on hook, working in back of last fpdtr, dc in next 3 dc, ch 2, join in beg pc. Fasten off.

Rnd 4: Join light pink with sl st in ch sp after any pc, 2 sc in same sp, *sc in each st across to next ch-2 sp, 2 sc in ch-2 sp, ch 3, 2 sc in next ch-2 sp, rep from * 3 times, sc in each st across to next ch-2 sp, 2 sc in ch-2 sp, ch 3, join in back lp of beg sc. Fasten off.

Rnd 5: Working in **back lps** *(see Stitch Guide)* only, join baby yellow in last joining sl st, ch 3, *dc in each st across to ch-2 sp, 5 dc in ch-2 sp *(corner made)*, rep from * 3 times, dc in each st to beg ch-3, join in 3rd ch of beg ch-3. Fasten off.

Rnd 6: Join lavender with sl st in 3rd dc of any corner, ch 1, 2 sc in same dc *(corner made)*, ***fpdc** *(see Stitch Guide)* around 3rd dc in corner, sk st in back, sc in next st, [dc in front lp of st of rnd 4, sk st in back, sc in next st] 6 times, fpdc around 3rd dc in corner, sk st in back, 2 sc in next st, rep from * 3 times, fpdc around middle dc in corner, sk st in back, sc in next st, [dc in front lp of st of rnd 4, sk st in back, sc in next st] 6 times,

American School of Needlework • Berne, Indiana 46711 • DRGnetwork.com   Beautiful Borders Baby Blankets • **3**

fpdc around middle dc in corner, sk st in back, join in beg sc.

Rnd 7: Ch 1, 2 sc in same st, *2 sc in next st, sc in next 15 sts, 2 sc in next st, rep from * 3 times, 2 sc in next st, sc in next 15 sts, join in beg sc. Fasten off.

Block Strip Assembly

Hold 2 Blocks with RS tog, with size G hook and lavender, sl st through back lps only across 1 side. Join rem Blocks in same manner, making 4 strips of 6 Blocks each.

Block Strip Edging

Hold 1 Block Strip with RS facing, with size G hook, join lavender with sc in first sc of any 2-sc group on 1 long side, sc in each of 114 sc across, skipping joinings, ch 2, working across next side, sc in each of next 19 sc, ch 2, working across next side, sc in each of next 114 sc, ch 2, working across next side, sc in each of next 19 sc, ch 2, join in beg sc. *(266 sc)*
Rep on rem Block Strips.

Ring Strip
Make 3.

First ring
With size H hook and baby blue, ch 10, join with sl st in first ch to form ring, ch 2, 24 hdc in ring, join in first hdc. *(24 hdc)*

2nd ring
With size H hook and baby yellow, ch 10, insert beg end of ch through First Ring, join with sl st in first ch to form ring, ch 2, 24 hdc in ring, join in first hdc. *(24 hdc)*

3rd ring
With size H hook and pastel green, ch 10, insert beg end of ch through last Ring made, join with sl st in first ch to form ring, ch 2, 24 hdc in ring, join in first hdc. *(24 hdc)*

4th ring
With size H hook and light pink, ch

10, insert beg end of ch through last Ring made, join with sl st in first ch to form ring, ch 2, 24 hdc in ring, join in first hdc. *(24 hdc)*

5th–28th rings
Work same as 4th Ring, working rem Rings in same color sequence as first 4 Rings.

Ring Strip Edging
Note: Place joining of each Ring under following Ring.

Rnd 1: Hold 1 Ring Strip with RS facing and First Ring to right, with size G hook, join lavender with sl st in first hdc of side of 2nd Ring after interlocking of First Ring, ch 1, sc in same hdc, sc in next 3 hdc, *sc in next 4 hdc on next Ring, rep from * 22 times, [sc in next 4 hdc, 2 sc in next hdc] twice on next Ring, sc in next 4 hdc, **working across next side, sk next 8 hdc on Ring, sc in next 4 hdc on next Ring, rep from ** 22 times, [sc in next 4 hdc, 2 sc in next hdc] twice on next Ring, sc in next 4 hdc, join in beg sc.

Rnd 2: Ch 1, sc in same sc, sc in next 108 sc, ch 2, sc in next 6 sc, ch 2, sc in next 114 sc, ch 2, sc in next 6 sc, ch 2, sc in last 5 sc, join in beg sc. Fasten off.

Strip Assembly
Hold 1 Block Strip and 1 Ring Strip with RS tog and 1 long edge at top, with size G hook and lavender, and working in back lps only, sl st across side, beg and ending in ch-2 sps at ends.
Join rem Block Strips and Ring Strips in same manner, alternating placement of Strips.

Outer Border
Rnd 1: Hold piece with RS facing, with size H hook, join lavender with sl st in ch-2 sp in right-hand corner, ch 1, 3 sc in same sp *(corner made)*, working around outer edge of piece, sc in each st, 2 sc in each ch-2 sp of joinings and 3 sc in each rem outer corner ch-2 sp, join in beg sc. Fasten off.
Note: On the following rnd, it is extremely important that when changing colors, the old yarn

be kept to the front; otherwise, pattern will not work properly. Also, because you are working with 4 different colors, occasionally the yarns will need to be unwound. To make it easier to unwind the yarns, place each yarn in a snug-fitting plastic bag; turn 1 bag at a time until yarn is unwound.

Rnd 2: With H hook, join baby blue with sc in 3rd sc of any corner, ch 10, sk next 3 sc, sc in next sc, ch 10, drop lp from hook, keep ch to front of work, join baby yellow with sc in first sk sc, ch 10, sc in next unused sc on rnd 1, ch 10, drop lp from hook, keep ch to front of work, join pastel green with sc in 2nd sk sc of first 3 sk sc, ch 10, sc in next unused sc on rnd 1, ch 10, drop lp from hook, keep ch to front of work, join light pink with sc in 3rd sk ch of first 3 sk chs, ch 10, sc in next unused sc on rnd 1, ch 10, drop lp from hook, keep ch to front of work, *insert hook in dropped baby blue lp, sc in next unused sc on rnd 1, ch 10, drop lp from hook, keep ch to front of work, insert hook in dropped baby yellow lp, sc in next unused sc on rnd 1, ch 10, drop lp from hook, keep ch to front of work, insert hook in dropped pastel green lp, sc in next unused sc on rnd 1, ch 10, drop lp from hook, keep ch to front of work, insert hook in dropped light pink lp, sc in next unused sc on rnd 1, ch 10, drop lp from hook, keep ch to front of work, rep from * across to 2nd sc of next corner, insert hook in dropped baby blue lp, sc in 2nd sc of corner, ch 10, drop lp from hook, keep ch to front of work, insert hook in dropped baby yellow lp, sc in same sc as baby blue sc made, ch 10, drop lp from hook, keep ch to front of work, insert hook in dropped pastel green lp, sc in same sc as previous 2 sc made, ch 10, drop lp from hook, keep ch to front of

work, insert hook in dropped light pink lp, sc in same sc as previous 3 sc made, ch 10, drop lp from hook, keep ch to front of work, working in color sequence as established, **insert hook in next dropped lp, sc in next unused sc on rnd 1, ch 10, drop lp from hook, keep ch to front of work, rep from ** across to 2nd sc of next corner, insert hook in next dropped lp, sc in 2nd sc of corner, ch 10, drop lp from hook, keep ch to front of work, insert hook in next dropped lp, sc in same sc as last sc made, ch 10, drop lp from hook, keep ch to front of work, insert hook in next dropped lp, sc in same sc as previous 2 sc made, 10, drop lp from hook, keep ch to front of work, insert hook in next dropped lp, sc in same sc as previous 3 sc made, ch 10, drop lp from hook, keep ch to front of work, ***insert hook in next dropped lp, sc in next unused sc on rnd 1, ch 10, drop lp from hook, keep ch to front of work, rep from *** across to 2nd sc of next corner, insert hook in next dropped lp, sc in 2nd sc of corner, ch 10, drop lp from hook, keep ch to front of work, insert hook in next dropped lp, sc in same sc as last sc made, ch 10, drop lp from hook, keep ch to front of work, insert hook in next dropped lp, sc in same sc as previous 2 sc made, 10, drop lp from hook, keep ch to front of work, insert hook in next dropped lp, sc in same sc as previous 3 sc made, ch 10, drop lp from hook, keep ch to front of work, ****insert hook in next dropped lp , sc in next unused sc on rnd 1, ch

(Precious Moments, cont.)

10, drop lp from hook, keep ch to front of work, rep from **** across to 2nd sc of next corner, insert hook in next dropped lp, sc in 2nd sc of corner, ch 10, drop lp from hook, keep ch to front of work, insert hook in next dropped lp,

sc in same sc as last sc made, ch 10, drop lp from hook, keep ch to front of work, insert hook in next dropped lp, sc in same sc as previous 2 sc made, 10, drop lp from hook, keep ch to front of work, insert hook in next dropped lp, sc in same sc as previous 3 sc made, ch 10, drop lp from hook, keep ch to front of work, insert hook in dropped baby blue lp, ch 10, join in beg baby blue sc, fasten off, insert hook in dropped baby yellow lp, ch 10, join in beg baby yellow lp, fasten off, insert hook in dropped pastel green lp, ch 10, join in beg pastel green sc, fasten off, insert hook in dropped light pink lp, ch 10, join in beg light pink lp, fasten off.

Rnd 3: Hold piece with RS facing and 1 short end at top, with size H hook, join lavender with sl st in first baby blue ch-10 lp at top of left-hand side, ch 1, sc in same lp, sc in each rem ch-10 lp around, join in beg sc.

Rnd 4: Ch 4 *(see Pattern Notes)*, [sk next sc, dc in next sc, ch 1] 56 times, sk next sc, (dc, ch 1) twice in each of next 3 sc, [sk next sc, dc in next sc, ch 1] 60 times, sk next sc, (dc, ch 1) twice in each of next 3 sc, [sk next sc, dc in next sc, ch 1] 58 times, sk next sc, (dc, ch 1) twice in each of next 3 sc, [sk next sc, dc in next sc, ch 1] 60 times, sk next sc, (dc, ch 1) twice in each of next 3 sc, sk next sc, dc in next sc, ch 1, join in 3rd ch of beg ch-4.

Rnd 5: Sl st in next ch-1 sp, **beg shell** *(see Special Stitches)* in same sp, sc in next ch sp, ***shell** *(see Special Stitches)* in next ch sp, rep from * around, join in beg sc.

Rnd 6: Sl st in next ch-1 sp, ch 1, sc in same sp, *ch 1, (dc, ch 3, sl st in 3rd ch from hook, ch 1, dc) in next dc, ch 1, sc in next ch-1 sp, sk next dc, sc in next sc,** sc in next ch-1 sp, rep from * around, ending last rep at **, join in beg sc. Fasten off. ●

Skill Level

 EXPERIENCED

Finished Size

36 x 42 inches

Materials

- Red Heart Baby Econo medium (worsted) weight yarn (7 oz/675 yds/198g per skein):
  - 2 skeins #1 white
  - 1 skein each #1224 baby yellow, #802 baby blue, #1722 light pink, #1680 pastel green
- Size G/6/4mm crochet hook or size needed to obtain gauge
- Tapestry needle

Gauge

5 dc = 1 inch

Pattern Notes

Weave in ends as work progresses.

Join rounds with a slip stitch unless otherwise stated.

Chain-3 at beginning of double crochet round counts as first double crochet unless otherwise stated.

Special Stitches

Cluster (cl): Holding back last lp of each tr on hook, 3 tr in indicated st, yo, draw through all 4 lps on hook.

Beginning shell (beg shell): Ch 3, (dc, ch 2, 2 dc) in indicated sp.

Shell: (2 dc, ch 2, 2 dc) in indicated sp.

Cross-stitch (cross-st): Sk indicated st, fpdc in next st, working in front of fpdc just made, fpdc in sk st.

Double crochet cluster (dc cl): Holding back last lp of each dc on hook, 3 dc in indicated sp, yo, draw through all 4 lps on hook.

Instructions

Ring Block

Make 14.

First ring

Rnd 1: With pastel green, ch 16, join with sl st in first ch to form a ring, ch 1 *(counts as a sc)*, 23 sc in ring, join in beg ch 1. *(24 sc)*

Rnd 2: Ch 1, sc in same sc, sc in each sc around, join in beg sc. Fasten off.

2nd ring

Rnd 1: With baby yellow, ch 10, insert beg end of ch through First Ring, join with sl st in first ch to form ring, ch 1, 24 sc in ring, join in first hdc. *(24 sc)*

Rnd 2: Ch 1, sc in each of 11 sc, (hdc, dc, hdc) in next sc *(corner made)*, sc in each of next 12 sc, join in beg sc. Fasten off.

3rd ring

With baby blue, work same as First Ring .

4th ring

With baby blue, work same as 2nd Ring. *(corner ring)*

5th ring

Work same as First Ring.

6th ring

Work same as 2nd Ring. *(corner ring)*

7th ring

Work same as 3rd Ring.

8th ring

Work same as 4th Ring, joining to 7th Ring and to First Ring. *(corner ring)*

Edging

Note: Place joining of each Ring under following Ring.

Rnd 1: Working in **back lps** *(see Stitch Guide)* only, join white with sl st in dc of any corner on First Ring, **ch 3** *(see Pattern Notes)*, 2 dc in same dc *(beg corner made)*, *dc in each of next 6 sc on side of next Ring, dc in next 4 sc before next corner on next Ring, dc in next hdc, 3 dc in next dc *(corner made)*, dc in next hdc, dc in each of next 4 sc, rep from * twice, dc in each of next 6 sc on side of next ring, dc in next 4 sc on next ring, dc in next hdc, join in 3rd ch of beg ch-3.

Rnd 2: Ch 1, sc in same ch as joining, sc in each of next 8 sts, *sk next 2 sts, [cl *(see Special Stitches)* in next st, ch 1 tightly, ch 6] twice; cl in next st, ch 1 tightly, sk next 2 sts, sc in each of next 12 sts, rep from * 3 times, sk next 2 sts, [cl in next st, ch 1 tightly, ch 6] twice; cl in next st, ch 1 tightly, sk next 2 sts, sc in last 3 sts, join in beg sc.

Rnd 3: Ch 3, dc in each of next 2 sts, working in front of 3 sts just made, dc in same ch as beg ch-3 made, *[sk next 2 sts, dc in next st, working behind dc just made, dc in 2 sk sts, dc in same st as first dc made] twice, (5 sc, dc) in

next ch-6 sp, (dc, 5 sc) in next ch-6 sp, [sk next cl, dc in next 3 sts, working in front of 3 dc just made, dc in same st as first dc was made] twice, rep from * 3 times, join in 3rd ch of beg ch-3.

Rnd 4: Ch 1, sc in same ch as joining, *sc in each of next 2 sts, sk next 2 dc, sc in each of next 3 dc, sk next dc, sc in each of next 8 sts, (2 sc, hdc) in next dc, (hdc, 2 sc) in next dc, sc in each of next 8 sts, sk next dc, sc in next dc, rep from * 3 times, sc in each of next 2 dc, sk next 2 dc, sc in each of next 3 sts, sk next dc, sc in each of next 8 sts, (2 sc, hdc) in next dc, (hdc, 2 sc) in next dc, sc in each of next 8 sts, sk next dc, join in beg sc.

Rnd 5: Ch 1, sc in same sc, sc in each of next 16 sts, ch 2, [sc in each of next 28 sts, ch 2] 3 times, sc in each of last 11 sts, join in beg sc. Fasten off.

White Block

Make 6.

Rnd 1: With white, ch 4, join with sl st in first ch to form ring, ch 3, 3 dc in ring, [ch 2, 4 dc in ring] 3 times; join with hdc in 3rd ch of beg ch-3.

Rnd 2: Beg shell *(see Special Stitches)* in same sp, *[**cross-st** *(see Special Stitches)* in next 2 sts] twice, **shell** *(see Special Stitches)* in next ch-3 sp, rep from * twice, [cross-st in next 2 sts] twice, join in 3rd ch of beg ch-3.

Rnd 3: Sl st in next dc and in next ch-2 sp, beg shell in same sp, *cross-st in next 2 sts, dc in each of next 4 sts, cross-st in next 2 sts, shell in next ch-2 sp, rep from * 3 times, cross-st in next 2 sts, dc in each of next 4 sts, cross-st in next 2 sts, join in 3rd ch of beg ch-3.

Rnd 4: Sl st in next dc and in next ch-2 sp, beg shell in same sp, *cross-st in next 2 sts, dc in each of next 2 sts, [cross-st in next 2 sts] twice, dc in each of next 2 sts, cross-st in next 2 sts**, shell in ch-2 sp of next shell, rep from * 4 times, ending last rep at **, join in 3rd ch of beg ch-3.

Rnd 5: Sl st in next dc and in next ch-2 sp, beg shell in same sp, *[cross-st in next 2 sts, dc in each of next 2 sts] twice, [dc in each of next 2 sts, cross-st in next 2 sts] twice**, shell in ch-2 sp of next shell, rep from * 4 times, ending last rep at **, join in 3rd ch of beg ch-3.

Rnd 6: Sl st in next dc and in next ch-2 sp, beg shell in same sp, *[cross-st in next 2 sts, dc in each of next 2 sts] twice, [cross-st in next 2 sts] twice, [dc in each of next 2 sts, cross-st in next 2 sts]**, shell in ch-2 sp of next shell, rep from * 4 times, ending last rep at **, join in 3rd ch of beg ch-3.

Rnd 7: Sl st in next ch sp, ch 3, 3 dc in same sp *(beg corner made)*, *[cross-st in next 2 sts, dc in each of next 2 sts] 3 times, [dc in each of next 2 sts, cross-st in next 2 sts] 3 times, 4 dc in next ch-2 sp *(corner made)*, rep from * 3 times, [cross-st in next 2 sts, dc in each of next 2 sts] 3 times, [dc in each of next 2 sts, cross-st in next 2 sts] 3 times, join in 3rd ch of beg ch-3.

Rnd 8: Ch 1, sc in same ch as joining, sc in each st around; join in beg sc.

Rnd 9: Ch 1, sc in same sc, sc in next sc, ch 2 *(corner made)*, *sc in each sc across to next corner, ch 2 *(corner made)*, rep from * twice, sc in each sc to beg sc, join in beg sc.

Assembly

Referring to photo for placement and working in **back lps** *(see Stitch Guide)* only, sl st all Blocks tog.

Edging

Rnd 1: Working in back lps *(see Stitch Guide)* only, join white with sl st in any st on First Ring, **ch 3** *(see Pattern Notes)*, dc in each of next 5 sts, *dc in each of next 4 sc before corner on next Ring, dc in next hdc, 3 dc in next dc *(corner made)*, dc in next hdc, dc in each of next 4 sc **, dc in each of next 6 sts on next Ring, rep from * 3 times, ending last rep at **, join in 3rd ch of beg ch-3.

Rnd 2: Ch 1, sc in same ch as joining, sc in each of next 8 sts, *sk next 2 sts, [**cl** *(see Special Stitches)* in next st, ch 1 tightly, ch 6] twice; cl in next st, ch 1 tightly, sk next 2 sts, sc in each of next 12 sts, rep from * twice, sk next 2 sts, [cl in next st, ch 1 tightly, ch 6] twice; cl in next st, ch 1 tightly, sk next 2 sts, sc in last 3 sts, join in beg sc.

Rnd 3: Ch 3, dc in each of next 2 sts, working in front of 3 sts just made, dc in same ch as beg ch-3 made, *[sk next 2 sts, dc in next st, working behind dc just made, dc in 2 sk sts, dc in same st as first dc made, inserting hook in st before first dc] twice, (5 sc, dc) in next ch-6 sp, (dc, 5 sc) in next ch-6 sp, sk next cl **, [dc in next 3 sts, working in front of 3 dc just made, dc in same st as first dc made] twice, rep from * 3 times, ending last rep at **, [dc in next 3 sts, working in front of 3 dc just made, dc in same st as first dc made, join in 3rd ch of beg ch-3.

Rnd 4: Sl st in each of next 2 sts, ch 1, sc in same st, *ch 5, sk next 4 sts, sc in next st, rep from * around, ch 2, join with dc in beg sc.

Rnd 5: Ch 1, sc in sp formed by joining dc, *[tr, ch 1] 7 times in next ch-5 sp, tr in same sp, sc in next ch-5 sp, rep from * 11 times, ch 6 *(corner made)*, sc in next ch-5 sp, **[tr, ch 1] 7 times in next ch-5 sp, tr in same sp, sc in next ch-5 sp, rep from ** 14 times, ch 6 *(corner made)*, sc in next ch-5 sp, ***[tr, ch 1] 7 times in next ch-5 sp, tr in same sp, sc in next ch-5 sp, rep from *** 11 times, ch 6 *(corner made)*, sc in next ch-5 sp, ****[tr, ch 1] 7 times in next ch-5 sp, tr in same sp, sc in next ch-5 sp, rep from **** 14 times, ch 6 *(corner made)*, join in beg sc.

Rnd 6: Sl st in next tr, ch 1, sc in same st, sc in next ch-1 sp, ch 2, sc in next ch-1 sp, ch 2, **bpdc** *(see Stitch Guide)* around next tr, **bptr** *(see*

Stitch Guide) around next tr ch 4, dc in 4th ch from hook, ch 1 tightly, bptr around next tr, bpdc around next tr, ch 2, sc in next ch-1 sp, ch 2, sc in next ch-1 sp, sc in next tr, *sc in next tr, sc in next ch-1 sp, ch 2, sc in next ch-1 sp, ch 2, bpdc around next tr, bptr around next tr, ch 4, dc in 4th ch from hook, ch 1 tightly, bptr around next tr, bpdc around next tr, ch 2, sc in next ch-1 sp, ch 2, sc in next ch-1 sp, sc in next tr, rep from * 10 times, (sc, {dc, ch 1} 4 times, dc, sc) in next corner ch-6 sp, **sc in next tr, sc in next ch-1 sp, ch 2, sc in next ch-1 sp, ch 2, bpdc around next tr, bptr around next tr, ch 4, dc in 4th ch from hook, ch 1 tightly, bptr around next tr, bpdc around next tr, ch 2, sc in next ch-1 sp, ch 2, sc in next ch-1 sp, sc in next tr, rep from ** 14 times, (sc, {dc, ch 1} 4 times, dc, sc) in next corner ch-6 sp, ***sc in next tr, sc in next ch-1 sp, ch 2, sc in next ch-1 sp, ch 2, bpdc around next tr, bptr around next tr, ch 4, dc in 4th ch from hook, ch 1 tightly, bptr around next tr, bpdc around next tr, ch 2, sc in next ch-1 sp, ch 2, sc in next ch-1 sp, sc in next tr, rep from *** 10 times, (sc, {dc, ch 1} 4 times, dc, sc) in next corner ch-6 sp, ****sc in next tr, sc in next ch-1 sp, ch 2, sc in next ch-1 sp, ch 2, bpdc around next tr, bptr around next tr, ch 4, dc in 4th ch from hook, ch 1 tightly, bptr around next tr, bpdc around next tr, ch 2, sc in next ch-1 sp, ch 2, sc in next ch-1 sp, sc in next tr, rep from **** 4 times, (sc, {dc, ch 1} 4 times, dc, sc) in next corner ch-6 sp, join in beg sc.

Rnd 7: Sl st in next st, ch 1, sc in same st, *sc in next ch sp, ch 2, sc in next ch sp, ch 2, sc in next ch-1 sp *(base of dc)*, ch 4, **dc cl** *(see Special Stitches)* in next ch-4 sp, ch 6, sl st in 3rd ch from hook, ch 3, sl st in 3rd ch from hook, ch 4, sc in next tight ch-1 sp, [ch 2, sc in next ch-2 sp] twice, sc in next sc, sk 2 sc, sc in next sc, rep from * 10 times, ch

2, sc in next ch sp, ch 2, sc in next ch-1 sp *(base of dc)*, ch 4, dc cl in next ch-4 sp, ch 6, sl st in 3rd ch from hook, ch 3, sl st in 3rd ch from hook, ch 4, sc in next tight ch-1 sp, [ch 2, sc in next ch-2 sp] twice, sc in next sc, [bpdc around next dc, ch 4, sl st in 3rd ch from hook, ch 1] 4 times, bpdc around last dc on corner, sk next 2 sc, sc in next sc, **sc in next ch sp, ch 2, sc in next ch sp, ch 2, sc in next ch-1 sp *(base of dc)*, ch 4, dc cl in next ch-4 sp, ch 6, sl st in 3rd ch from hook, ch 3, sl st in 3rd ch from hook, ch 4, sc in next tight ch-1 sp, [ch 2, sc in next ch-2 sp] twice, sc in next sc, sk next 2 sc, sc in next sc, rep from ** 13 times, ch 2, sc in next ch sp, ch 2, sc in next ch-1 sp *(base of dc)*, ch 4, dc cl in next ch-4 sp, ch 6, sl st in 3rd ch from hook, ch 3, sl st in 3rd ch from hook, ch 4, sc in next tight ch-1 sp, [ch 2, sc in next ch-2 sp] twice, sc in next sc, ***sc in next ch sp, ch 2, sc in next ch sp, ch 2, sc in next ch-1 sp *(base of dc)*, ch 4, dc cl in next ch-4 sp, ch 6, sl st in 3rd ch from hook, ch 3, sl st in 3rd ch from hook, ch 4, sc in next tight ch-1 sp, [ch 2, sc in next ch-2 sp] twice, sc in next sc, sk 2 sc, sc in next sc, rep from *** 10 times, ch 2, sc in next ch sp, ch 2, sc in next ch-1 sp *(base of dc)*, ch 4, dc cl in next ch-4 sp, ch 6, sl st in 3rd ch from hook, ch 3, sl st in 3rd ch from hook, ch 4, sc in next tight ch-1 sp, [ch 2, sc in next ch-2 sp] twice, sc in next sc, ****sc in next ch sp, ch 2, sc in next ch sp, ch 2, sc in next ch-1 sp *(base of dc)*, ch 4, dc cl in next ch-4 sp, ch 6, sl st in 3rd ch from hook, ch 3, sl st in 3rd ch from hook, ch 4, sc in next tight ch-1 sp, [ch 2, sc in next ch-2 sp] twice, sc in next sc, sk 2 sc, sc in next sc, rep from **** 13 times, ch 2, sc in next ch sp, ch 2, sc in next ch-1 sp *(base of dc)*, ch 4, dc cl in next ch-4 sp, ch 6, sl st in 3rd ch from hook, ch 3, sl st in 3rd ch from hook, ch 4, sc in next tight ch-1 sp, [ch 2, sc in next ch-2 sp] twice, join in beg sc. Fasten off. ●

Precious in Pink

Skill Level
 **EXPERIENCED**

Finished Size
46 x 30 inches

Materials
- Red Heart Baby Econo medium (worsted) weight yarn (7 oz/675 yds/198g per skein):
  - 3 skeins #1722 light pink
- Size G/6/4mm crochet hook or size needed to obtain gauge
- Tapestry needle

Gauge
5 dc = 1 inch

Pattern Notes
Weave in ends as work progresses.
Join rounds with a slip stitch unless otherwise stated.
Chain-3 at beginning of double crochet round counts as first double crochet unless otherwise stated.

Special Stitches
Double crochet cluster (dc cl): Holding back last lp of each dc on hook, 2 dc in indicated st, yo, draw through all 3 lps on hook.
Back post double crochet cluster (bpdc cl): Holding back last lp of each bpdc on hook, 2 bptr around indicated st, yo, draw through all 3 lps on hook.
Treble crochet cluster (tr cl): [Yo twice, insert hook in indicated st, yo, draw lp through, {yo, draw through 2 lps on hook} twice] twice, yo and draw through all 3 lps on hook.

Rice stitch (rice st): Ch 3, hdc in in 3rd ch from hook.

Instructions

First Half
Row 1 (RS): Ch 179, dc in 4th ch from hook *(beg 3 sk chs count as a dc)*, dc each ch across, turn. *(177 dc)*
Row 2: Ch 3 *(see Pattern Notes)*, *****fpdc** *(see Stitch Guide)* around each of next 5 dc, **bpdc** *(see Stitch Guide)* around each of next 5 dc, rep from * 16 times, fpdc around each of next 5 dc, dc in 3rd ch of beg 3 sk chs, turn.
Row 3: Ch 3, *fpdc around each of next 5 sts, bpdc around each of next 5 sts, rep from * 33 times, fpdc around each of next 5 sts, dc in 3rd ch of turning ch-3, turn.
Rows 4–38: Rep row 3. Fasten off.

2nd Half
Row 1: Hold First Half with RS facing and foundation ch at top; join yarn with sl st in unused lp of first ch, *fpdc around each of next 5 dc on row 1 of First Half, bpdc around each of next 5 dc on row 1, rep from * 16 times, fpdc around each of next 5 dc, dc in unused lp of last ch, turn.
Rnds 2–37: Rep rnds 2–37 of First Half. Do not fasten off.

Border
Rnd 1: Ch 1, working across next side in sps formed by edge dc and turning chs at ends of rows, sc in each row, ch 2, working across next side, sk first dc, sc in each st across to last dc, ch 2, sk last dc, working across next side in sps formed by edge dc and turning chs at ends of rows, sc in each row, ch 2, working across next side, sk first dc, sc in each st across to last dc, ch 2, sk last dc, join in beg sc. *(500 sc)*

Rnd 2: Ch 2, dc in same sc *(beg dc cl made)*, [ch 1, sk next sc, **dc cl** *(see Special Stitches)* in next sc] 37 times, ch 1, (dc cl, ch 2) twice in next ch-2 sp, dc cl in same sp *(corner made)*, ch 1, dc cl in next sc, [ch 1, sk next sc, dc cl in next sc] 87 times, ch 1, (dc cl, ch 2) twice in next ch-2 sp, dc cl in same sp *(corner made)*, ch 1, cl in next sc, [ch 1, sk next sc, dc cl in next sc] 37 times, ch 1, (dc cl, ch 2) twice in nekxt ch-2 sp, dc cl in same sp *(corner made)*, ch 1, dc cl in next sc, [ch 1, sk next sc, dc cl in next sc] 87 times, ch 1, (dc cl, ch 2) twice in next ch-2 sp, dc cl in same sp *(corner made)*, join in first dc. Fasten off. *(8 ch-2 sps, 254 ch-1 sps, 264 dc cl)*

Rnd 3: Join yarn with sc in 2nd ch-2 sp of last corner made on previous rnd, *ch 3, sc in next ch-1 sp, sk next ch-1 sp, (dc, ch 1) twice in next dc cl, (tr, ch 1) twice in same dc cl, (dc, ch 1, dc) in same dc cl, sk next ch-1 sp, sc in next ch-1 sp, ch 3, sc in next ch-1 sp, rep from * 7 times, ch 3, sc in next ch-1 sp, **ch 3, sc in next ch-1 sp, sk next ch-1 sp, (dc, ch 1) twice in next dc cl, (tr, ch 1) twice in same dc cl, (dc, ch 1, dc) in same dc cl, sk next ch-1 sp, sc in next ch-1 sp, ch 3, sc in next ch-1 sp, rep from ** 17 times, ch

3, sc in next ch-1 sp, ***ch 3, sc in next ch-1 sp, sk next ch-1 sp, (dc, ch 1) twice in next dc cl, (tr, ch 1) twice in same dc cl, (dc, ch 1, dc) in same dc cl, sk next ch-1 sp, sc in next ch-1 sp, ch 3, sc in next ch-1 sp, rep from *** 7 times, ch 3, sc in next ch-1 sp, ****ch 3, sc in next ch-1 sp, sk next ch-1 sp, (dc, ch 1) twice in next dc cl, (tr, ch 1) twice in same dc cl, (dc, ch 1, dc) in same dc cl, sk next ch-1 sp, sc in next ch-1 sp, ch 3, sc in next ch-1 sp, rep from **** 17 times, ch 3 ◊, sc in next ch-1 sp, rep from * twice, ending last rep at ◊, join in beg sc.

Rnd 4: Sl st in next ch-3 sp, ch 1, 2 sc in same sp, *[{**bpdc cl** *(see Special Stitches)* around next st, **rice st** *(see Special Stitches)*} 3 times, **tr cl** *(see Special Stitches)* in next ch-1 sp, ch 4, sl st in top of tr cl just made, {rice st, bpdc cl around next st} 3 times, 2 sc in each of next 2 ch sps] 7 times, [bpdc cl around next st, rice st] 3 times, tr cl in next ch-1 sp, ch 4, sl st in top of tr cl just made, [rice st, bpdc cl around next st] 3 times, 2 sc in next ch sp, (dc, ch 1) 3 times in next sp, dc in same sp, 2 sc in next ch sp, [{bpdc cl around next st, rice st} 3 times, tr cl in next ch-1 sp, ch 4, sl st in top of tr cl just made, {rice st, bpdc cl around next st} 3 times, 2 sc in each of next 2 ch sps] 17 times, [bpdc cl around next st, rice st] 3 times, tr cl in next ch-1 sp, ch 4, sl st in top of tr cl just made, [rice st, bpdc cl around next st] 3 times, 2 sc in next ch sp, (dc, ch 1) 3 times in next sp, dc in same sp,** 2 sc in next ch sp, rep from * twice, ending last rep at **, join in beg sc.

Rnd 5: Ch 1, sc in same sc, *[sc in ch-3 of next rice st, rice st] 3 times, **fptr** *(see Stitch Guide)*

around first tr of next tr cl, (sc, ch 4, sl st in 4th ch from hook, ch 1, sc) in next ch-4 sp, fptr around 2nd tr of same tr cl, [rice st, sc in ch-3 sp of next rice st] 3 times, sk next sc, **sc dec** *(see Stitch Guide)* in next 2 sts, rep from * 7 times, **bpsc** *(see Stitch Guide)* around next dc, [rice st, bpdc cl around next dc] twice, rice st, bpsc around next dc, sc in next sc, **[sc in ch-3 of next rice st, rice st] 3 times, fptr around first tr of next tr cl, (sc, ch 4, sl st in 4th ch from hook, ch 1, sc) in next ch-4 sp, fptr around 2nd tr of same tr cl, [rice st, sc in ch-3 sp of next rice st] 3 times, sk next sc, sc dec in next 2 sts, rep from ** 17 times, bpsc around next dc, [rice st, bpdc cl around next dc] twice, rice st, bpsc around next dc, sc in next sc, ***[sc in ch-3 of next rice

st, rice st] 3 times, fptr around first tr of next tr cl, (sc, ch 4, sl st in 4th ch from hook, ch 1, sc) in next ch-4 sp, fptr around 2nd tr of same tr cl, [rice st, sc in ch-3 sp of next rice st] 3 times, sk next sc, sc dec in next 2 sts, rep from *** 7 times, bpsc around next dc, {rice st, bpdc cl around next dc} twice, rice st, bpsc around next dc, sc in next sc, ****[sc in ch-3 of next rice st, rice st] 3 times, fptr around first tr of next tr cl, (sc, ch 4, sl st in 4th ch from hook, ch 1, sc) in next ch-4 sp, fptr around 2nd tr of same tr cl, [rice st, sc in ch-3 sp of next rice st] 3 times, sk next sc, sc dec in next 2 sts, rep from **** 17 times, bpsc around next dc, {rice st, bpdc cl around next dc} twice, rice st, bpsc around next dc, sc in next sc. Fasten off. ●

Skill Level
 EXPERIENCED

Finished Size
40 x 48 inches

Materials
- Red Heart Baby Econo medium (worsted) weight yarn (7 oz/675 yds/198g per skein):
  - 3 skeins #1 white
  - 1 skein #1224 baby yellow
- Size G/6/4mm crochet hook or size needed to obtain gauge
- Tapestry needle

Gauge
5 sts = 1 inch

Pattern Notes
Weave in ends as work progresses.

Join rounds with a slip stitch unless otherwise stated.

Chain-3 at beginning of double crochet round counts as first double crochet unless otherwise stated.

Special Stitches
Double crochet cluster (dc cl): Holding back last lp of each dc on hook, work 2 dc in indicated st, yo, draw through all 3 lps on hook.

Front post tr cluster (fptr cl): Holding back last lp of each fptr on hook, fptr around each of 2 indicated sts, yo, draw through all 3 lps on hook.

Beg shell (beg shell): Ch 6, ({tr, ch 2} 4 times, tr) in same st.

Shell: ({Tr, ch 2} 5 times, tr} in indicated st.

Treble crochet cluster (tr cl): Holding back last lp of each tr on hook, work 3 tr in indicated st, yo, draw through all 4 lps on hook.

Instructions

Small Square
Make 18.

Rnd 1: With baby yellow, ch 4, join with sl st in first ch to form a ring, **ch 3** *(see Pattern Notes)*, 15 dc in ring, join in 3rd ch of beg ch-3. *(16 dc)*

Note: *Place marker around 2nd dc to left of beg ch-3.*

Rnd 2: Ch 1, sc in same ch as joining, ch 1, [sc in next dc, ch 1] 15 times, join in beg sc. Fasten off. *(16 sc, 16 ch-1 sps)*

Rnd 3: Join white with sl st in last ch-1 sp made on previous rnd, ch 1, 2 sc in same sp, **fptr** *(see Stitch Guide)* around marked dc on rnd 1, *2 sc in next ch-1 sp, fptr around next dc on rnd 1, rep from * 14 times, join in beg sc. Fasten off. *(16 fptr, 32 sc)*

Rnd 4: Join baby yellow with sc in any fptr, ch 3, **dc cl** *(see Special Stitches)* in 3rd ch from hook, *sc in next fptr, ch 3, dc cl in 3rd ch from hook, rep from * around, join in beg sc. Fasten off. *(16 sc, 16 dc cl)*

Rnd 5: Join white with sc in any sc, ch 4, *sc in next sc, ch 4, rep from * around, join in beg sc. *(16 sc, 16 ch-4 sps)*

Rnd 6: Sl st in next ch-4 sp, ch 3, (dc, ch 2, 2 dc) in same sp *(beg corner made)*, *ch 2, sc in next ch-4 sp, 5 hdc in next ch-4 sp, sc in next ch-4 sp, ch 2, (2 dc, ch 2, 2 dc) in next ch-4 sp *(corner made)*, rep from * twice, ch 2, sc in next ch-4 sp, 5 hdc in next ch-4 sp, sc in next ch-4 sp, ch 2, join in 3rd ch of beg ch-3.

Rnd 7: Ch 3, *dc in next dc, 4 dc in corner ch-2 sp *(corner made)*, dc in next 2 dc, 2 dc in next ch-2 sp, dc in next st, hdc in next st, sc in next 3 sts, hdc in next st, dc in next st, 2 dc in next ch-2 sp, dc in next st, rep from * 3 times, dc in next dc, 4 dc in corner ch-2 sp *(corner made)*, dc in next 2 dc, 2 dc in next ch-2 sp, dc in next st, hdc in next st, sc in next 3 sts, hdc in next st, dc in next st, 2 dc in next ch-2 sp, join in 3rd ch of beg ch-3. Fasten off.

Rnd 8: Working in **back lps** *(see Stitch Guide)* only, join baby yellow with sc in 3rd dc of any corner, *sc in next 8 sts, **fptr cl** *(see Special Stitches)* around first and 5th hdc of next corner on 2nd rnd below, on working rnd, sk st behind fptr cl, sc in next 9 sts, ch 2, sc in next st, rep from * twice, sc in next 8 sts, fptr cl around first and 5th hdc of next corner on 2nd rnd below, on working rnd, sk st behind fptr cl, sc in next 9 sts, ch 2, join in beg sc. *(76 sts, 4 ch-2 sps)*

Rnd 9: Ch 1, sc in same sc, *sc in next 18 sts, (sc, ch 2, sc) in next ch-2 sp, sc in next st, rep from * twice, sc in next 18 sts, (sc, ch 2, sc) in next ch-2 sp, join in beg sc. Fasten off. *(84 sc, 4 ch-2 sps)*

Rnd 10: Join white with sc in any ch-2 sp, ch 2, sc in same sp, *sc in each sc across, (sc, ch 2, sc) in

next ch sp, rep from * 3 times, sc in each st across, join in beg sc. *(92 sc, 4 ch-2 sps)*

Rnd 11: Sl st in next ch-2 sp, ch 1, (sc, ch 2, sc) in same sp, *[tr in next sc, sc in next sc] 11 times, tr in next st, (sc, ch 2, sc) in next ch-2 sp, rep from * twice, [tr in next sc, sc in next sc] 11 times, tr in next st, join in beg sc. *(48 tr, 52 sc, 4 ch-2 sps)*

Rnd 12: Ch 1, sc in same sc, *(sc, ch 2, sc) in next corner ch-2 sp, sc in each st across to next corner ch-2 sp, rep from * 3 times, join in beg sc. Fasten off. *(108 sc, 4 ch-2 sps)*

Large Square

Row 1: With white, ch 84, sc in 2nd ch from hook, *tr in next ch, sc in next ch, rep from * across, turn. *(83 sts)*

Row 2: Ch 1, sc in each st across, turn.

Row 3: Ch 1, sc in first 2 sts, *tr in next st, sc in next st, rep from * across to last sc, sc in last sc, turn.

Row 4: Rep row 2.

Row 5: Ch 1, sc in first sc, *tr in next st, sc in next st, rep from * across, turn.

Rows 6–109: [Rep rows 2–5 consecutively] 26 times.

Rows 110–112: Rep rows 2–4. Fasten off.

Edging

Rnd 1: Hold piece with RS facing, join baby yellow with sl st in first sc of row 112, ch 1, sc in same sc, sc in each of next 82 sc across, ch 2, working across next side in ends of rows, sc in each row, ch 2, working across next side in unused lps of beg ch, sc in each of next 83 chs across, ch 2, working across next side in ends of rows, sc in each row, ch 2, join in beg sc. Fasten off. *(390 sc, 4 ch-2 sps)*

Rnd 2: Join white with sl st in any ch-2 sp, ch 1, 4 sc in same sp *(corner made)*, sc in each sc across to next ch-2 sp, *4 sc in ch-2 sp

(corner made), sc in each sc to next ch-2 sp, rep from * twice, join in beg sc. Fasten off. *(406 sc)*

Assembly

Join Small Squares tog having 5 Squares across top and bottom and 4 Squares at each side, leaving center open. With white, sl st squares tog across 1 side, beg and ending with sl sts in each of 2 corner chs on either end of side. Join rem Small Squares in same manner. Join Large Square in center of Small Squares in same manner.

Border

Rnd 1: Hold piece with RS facing and 1 short end at top; join white with sc in first sc in right corner, *sc in each st across to next outer corner ch-2 sp, 3 sc in corner ch-2 sp *(corner made)*, rep from * 3 times, join in beg sc. *(406 sc)*

Rnd 2: Sl st in next 3 sc, **beg shell** *(see Special Stitches)* in same sc, [sk next 3 sc, sc in next sc, sk next 3 sc, **shell** *(see Special Stitches)*] 16 times, sk next 3 sc, sc in next st, sk next 3 sc, shell in next sc, sk next 4 sc, sc in next sc, sk next 2 sc, shell in next sc, [sk next 3 sc, sc in next sc, sk next 3 sc, shell in next sc] 21 times, sk next 3 sc, sc in next sc, sk next 4 sc, shell in next sc, [sk next 3 sc, sc in next sc, sk next 3 sc, shell in next sc] 17 times, sk next 4 sc, sc in next sc, sk next 2 sc, shell in next sc, [sk next 3 sc, sc in next sc, sk next 3 sc, shell in next st] 21 times, sk next 3 sc, sc in next sc, join in 4th ch of beg ch-6. *(80 shells)*

Rnd 3: Sl st in next ch-2 sp, ch 1, 2 sc in same sp, *2 sc in each of next 2 ch-1 sps, [ch 4, sc in next ch-1 sp] twice, [sc in next ch-1 sp, ch 4] twice, 2 sc in each of next 3 ch-1 sps, sk next tr, sc in next sc, 2 sc in next ch-1 sp, rep from * 38 times, 2 sc in each of next 2 ch-1 sps, [ch 4, sc in next ch-1 sp] twice, [sc in next ch-1 sp, ch 4]

twice, 2 sc in each of next 3 ch-1 sps, sk next tr, sc in next sc, join in beg sc.

Rnd 4: Sl st in next sc, ch 1, sc in same sc, *sc in next 4 sts, 2 sc in next ch-4 sp, ch 4, sc in next ch-4 sp, **tr cl** *(see Special Stitches)* around sc on 2nd rnd below, sc in next ch-4 sp, ch 4, sl st in next sc, sk next sc, sc in next sc, rep from * 38 times, sc in next 4 sts, 2 sc in next ch-4 sp, ch 4, sc in next ch-4 sp, tr cl around sc on 2nd rnd below, sc in next ch-4 sp, ch 4, sl st in next sc, sk next sc, join in beg sc.

Rnd 5: Ch 1, sc in same sc, *sc in next 6 sts, 2 sc in next ch-4 sp, tr in next ch-4 sp, ch 3, working behind tr just made, tr in same ch-4 sp after 2 sc already made, 2 sc in same ch-4 sp after first tr made, sc in next 7 sc, sk next sl st, sc in next sc, rep from * 38 times, sc in next 6 sts, 2 sc in next ch-4 sp, tr in next ch-4 sp, ch 3, working behind tr just made, tr in same ch-4 sp after 2 sc already made, 2 sc in same ch-4 sp after first tr made, sc in next 7 sc, sk next sl st, join in beg sc.

Rnd 6: Sl st in next st, ch 1, sc in same st, *[ch 3, dc cl in 3rd ch from hook, sk next 2 sts, sc in next st] twice, ch 3, dc cl in 3rd ch from hook, (sc, ch 4, dc in 4th ch from hook, sc) in next ch-3 sp, [ch 3, dc cl in 3rd ch from hook, sk next 2 sts, sc in next st] 3 times, sk next 2 sc, sc in next sc, rep from * 7 times, [ch 3, dc cl in 3rd ch from hook, sk next 2 sc, sc in next sc] twice, ch 3, dc cl in 3rd ch from hook, (sc, ch 4, dc in 4th ch from hook, sc) in next ch-3 sp, [ch 3, dc cl in 3rd ch from hook, sk next 2 sc, sc in next sc] 4 times, **[ch 3, dc cl in 3rd ch from hook, sk next 2 sc, sc in next sc] twice, ch 3, dc cl in 3rd ch from hook, (sc, ch 4, dc in 4th ch from hook, sc) in next ch-3 sp, [ch 3, dc cl

in 3rd ch from hook, sk next 2 sc, sc in next sc] 3 times, sk next 2 sc at base, sc in next sc, rep from ** 9 times, [ch 3, dc cl in 3rd ch from hook, sk next 2 sc, sc in next sc] twice, ch 3, dc cl in 3rd ch from hook, (sc, ch 4, dc in 4th ch from hook, sc) in next ch-3 sp, [ch 3, dc cl in 3rd ch from hook, sk next 2 sc, sc in next sc] 4 times, ***[ch 3, dc cl in 3rd ch from hook, sk next 2 sc, sc in next sc] twice, ch 3, dc cl in 3rd ch from hook, (sc, ch 4, dc in 4th ch from hook, sc) in next ch-3 sp, [ch 3, dc cl in 3rd

ch from hook, sk next 2 sc, sc in next sc] 3 times, sk next 2 sc, sc in next sc, rep from *** 7 times, [ch 3, dc cl in 3rd ch from hook, sk next 2 sc, sc in next sc] twice, ch 3, dc cl in 3rd ch from hook, (sc, ch 4, dc in 4th ch from hook, sc) in next ch-3 sp, [ch 3, dc cl in 3rd ch from hook, sk next 2 sc, sc in next sc] 4 times, ****[ch 3, dc cl in 3rd ch from hook, sk next 2 sc, sc in next sc] twice, ch 3, dc cl in 3rd ch from hook, (sc, ch 4, dc in 4th ch from hook, sc) in next ch-3 sp, [ch 3, dc cl in 3rd ch from hook, sk next 2 sc, sc in

next sc] 3 times, sk next 2 sc, sc in next st, rep from **** 9 times, [ch 3, dc cl in 3rd ch from hook, sk next 2 sc, sc in next sc] twice, ch 3, dc cl in 3rd ch from hook, (sc, ch 4, dc in 4th ch from hook, sc) in next ch-3 sp, [ch 3, dc cl in 3rd ch from hook, sk next 2 sc, sc in next sc] 3 times, ch 3, dc cl in 3rd ch from hook, sk next 2 sc, sc in next sc] twice, ch 3, dc cl in 3rd ch from hook, (sc, ch 4, dc in 4th ch from hook, sc) in next ch-3 sp, [ch 3, dc cl in 3rd ch from hook, sk next 2 sc, join in beg sc. Fasten off. ●

His & Hers Garden

Skill Level
 **EXPERIENCED**

Finished Sizes
28 x 39 inches

Materials
- Red Heart Soft Baby light (light worsted) weight yarn (7 oz/575 yds/198g per skein):
  - 3 skeins #7001 white
  - 1 skein each #7680 new mint, #7588 lilac, #7822 sky blue, #7730 bright pink
- Size G/6/4mm crochet hook or size needed to obtain gauge
- Tapestry needle

Gauge
Rnds 1 and 2 = 1 inch

Pattern Notes
Weave in ends as work progresses.

Join rounds with a slip stitch unless otherwise stated.

Chain-3 at beginning of double crochet round counts as first double crochet unless otherwise stated.

Chain-4 at beginning of double crochet round counts as first double crochet and chain-1 sp unless otherwise stated.

Special Stitches
Beginning popcorn (beg pc): Ch 3, 3 dc in indicated sp, drop lp from hook, insert hook from front to back in 3rd ch of beg ch-3, draw dropped lp through st.

Popcorn (pc): 4 dc in indicated sp, drop lp from hook, insert hook from front to back in first dc of 4-dc group, draw dropped lp through st.

Front post tr cluster (fptr cl): Holding back last lp of each fptr on hook, fptr around each of 4 indicated sts, yo, draw through all 5 lps on hook.

Beginning shell (beg shell): Ch 4, ({dc, ch 1} 4 times, dc) in sp indicated.

Shell: ({Dc, ch 1} 5 times, dc) in sp indicated.

Picot shell: (2 dc, ch 3, sl st in 3rd ch from hook—*picot made*, ch 1, 2 dc) in indicated sp.

Instructions

Multicolored Square
Make 6.

Mint block
Rnd 1: With white, ch 4, join with sl st to form a ring, **ch 3** *(see Pattern Notes)*, 15 dc in ring, join in 3rd ch of beg ch-3. *(16 dc)*

Rnd 2: Ch 1, **bpsc** *(see Stitch Guide)* around beg ch-3, ch 2, *bpsc around each of next 4 dc, ch 2, rep from * twice, bpsc around each of next 3 dc, join in beg sc. Fasten off. *(16 ch-2 sps, 16 bpsc)*

Rnd 3: Join new mint with sl st in any ch-2 sp, **beg pc** *(see Special Stitches)* in same sp, *ch 4, sc in each of next 3 ch-2 sps, ch 4, **pc** *(see Special Stitches)* in next ch-2 sp, rep from * twice, ch 4, sc in each of next 3 ch-2 sps, ch 4, join in beg pc. Fasten off. *(4 pc, 12 sc, 8 ch-4 sps)*

Rnd 4: Join white with sl st in ch-4 sp to left of any pc, ch 1, 4 sc in same sp, *ch 1, **fptr cl** *(see Special Stitches)* around next 4 bpsc on 2nd rnd below, ch 1, 4 sc in next ch-4 sp, ch 4, 4 sc in next ch-4 sp, rep from * twice, ch 1, fptr cl around next 4 bpsc on 2nd rnd below, ch 1, 4 sc in next ch-4 sp, ch 4, join in beg sc.

Rnd 5: Ch 1, sc in same sc, *sc in next 3 sc, **sc dec** *(see Stitch Guide)* in next 2 ch-1 sps, sc in next 4 sc, 4 sc in next ch-4 sp *(corner made)*, sc in next sc, rep from * twice, sc in next 3 sc, sc dec in next 2 ch-1 sps, sc in next 4 sc, 4 sc in next ch-4 sp *(corner made)*, join in beg sc. *(52 sc)*

Rnd 6: Ch 1, sc in same sc, *[ch 3, sk next sc, sc in next sc] 5 times, ch 5 *(corner made)*, sc in next sc, ch 3, sk next sc, sc in next sc, rep from * twice, [ch 3, sk next sc, sc in next sc] 5 times, ch 5 *(corner made)*, sc in next sc, ch 3, sk next sc, join in beg sc. Fasten off. *(28 sc, 4 ch-5 sps, 24 ch-3 sps)*

Lilac block
Rnds 1–5: Rep rnds 1–5 of Mint Block, working rnd 3 with lilac.

Rnd 6: Ch 1, sc in same sc, *[ch 3, sk next sc, sc in next sc] 5 times, ch 5 *(corner made)*, sc in next sc, ch 3, sk next sc, sc in next sc, rep from * once, [ch 3, sk next st, sc in next st] 5 times, ch 3, hold last Block made with RS facing and carefully matching sts, sl st in corresponding ch-5 corner on last Block made, ch 2, sc in next st on working Block, [ch 1, sl st in next ch-3 sp on last Block made, ch 1, sk next sc on working Block, sc in next sc] 5 times, ch 3, sl st in next ch-5 corner on last Block made, ch 2, sc in next sc on

 American School of Needlework • Berne, Indiana 46711 • DRGnetwork.com

working Block, ch 3, sk next sc, join in beg sc. Fasten off.

Blue block
Work same as Lilac Block, except work rnd 3 with sky blue and join to next adjacent unjoined side of Lilac Block.

Pink block
Work same as Lilac Block, except work rnd 3 with bright pink and join to Blue Block and Mint Block.

Edging
Join white with sl st in first ch-3 sp on any side, ch 1, 2 sc in same sp, * 2 sc in next 13 sps (including 2 corner sps), 4 sc in next outer corner ch-5 sp (corner made), 2 sc in next ch-3 sp, rep from * twice, 2 sc in next 13 sps (including 2 corner sps), 4 sc in next outer corner ch-5 sp (corner made), join in beg sc. Fasten off. (128 sc)

White Square
Make 6.

First block
Rnds 1 & 2: Rep rnds 1 and 2 of Mint Block.
Rnd 3: Sl st in next ch-2 sp, beg pc in same sp, *ch 4, sc in each of next 3 ch-2 sps, ch 4, pc next ch-2 sp, rep from * twice, ch 4, sc in each of next 3 ch-2 sps, ch 4, join in beg pc. Fasten off. (4 pc, 12 sc, 8 ch-4 sps)
Rnd 4: Sl st in next ch-4 sp, ch 1, 4 sc in same sp, *ch 1, fptr cl around next 4 bpsc on 2nd rnd below, ch 1, 4 sc in next ch-4 sp, ch 4, 4 sc in next ch-4 sp, rep from * twice, ch 1, fptr cl around next 4 bpsc on 2nd rnd below, ch 1, 4 sc in next ch-4 sp, ch 4, join in beg sc.
Rnd 5: Ch 1, sc in same sc, *sc in next 3 sc, sc dec in next 2 ch-1 sps, sc in next 4 sc, 4 sc in next ch-4 sp, sc in next sc, rep from * twice, sc in next 3 sc, sc dec in next 2 ch-1 sps, sc in next 4 sc, 4

sc in next ch-4 sp, join in beg sc. (52 sc)
Rnd 6: Ch 1, sc in same sc, *[ch 3, sk next sc, sc in next sc] 5 times, ch 5, sc in next sc, ch 3, sk next sc, sc in next sc, rep from * twice, [ch 3, sk next st, sc in next st] 5 times, ch 5, sc in next st, ch 3, sk next st, join in beg sc. Fasten off. (28 sc, 4 ch-5 sps, 24 ch-3 sps)

2nd block
Rnds 1–5: Rep rnds 1–5 of First Block.
Rnd 6: Ch 1, sc in same sc, *[ch 3, sk next sc, sc in next sc] 5 times, ch 5 (corner made), sc in next sc, ch 3, sk next sc, sc in next sc, rep from * once, [ch 3, sk next st, sc in next st] 5 times, ch 3, hold last Block made with RS facing and carefully matching sts, sl st in corresponding ch-5 corner on last Block made, ch 2, sc in next st on working Block, [ch 1, sl st in next ch-3 sp on last Block made, ch 1, sk next sc on working Block, sc in next sc] 5 times, ch 3, sl st in next ch-5 corner on last Block made, ch 2, sc in next sc on working Block, ch 3, sk next sc, join in beg sc. Fasten off.

3rd & 4th blocks
Work same as 2nd Block, joining 3rd Block to 2nd Block and 4th Block to 3rd and First Block.

Edging
Work same as Edging for Multicolored Square.

Assembly
Referring to photo for placement and working in **back lps** (see Stitch Guide) only, with white, sl st all Blocks tog.

Border
Rnd 1: Hold piece with RS facing and 1 short end at top, join white with sc in first sc in upper right-hand 4-sc corner, sc in next st, *ch 2, [sc in each of next

32 sts, **hdc dec** (see Stitch Guide) in joined sc on same Block and in next joined sc on next Block] twice, sc in each of next 32 sts, ch 2 (corner made), [sc in each of next 32 sts, hdc dec in next joined sc on same block and in next joined sc on next Block] 3 times **, sc in each of next 32 sts, ch 2 (corner made), rep from * once, ending rep at **, sc in each sc to beg sc, join in beg sc. Fasten off.
Rnd 2: Join lilac with sl st in first sc after ch-2 corner, **ch 4** (see Pattern Notes), sk next st, *dc in next st, ch 1, sk next st, dc in next st, rep from * to next corner ch-2 sp, ch 1, (dc, ch 1) 3 times in corner ch-2 sp, rep from * 3 times, join in 3rd ch of beg ch-4. Fasten off. (212 dc, 216 ch-1 sps)
Rnd 3: Join bright pink with sc in same ch as previous rnd joining, *[tr in sk sc on rnd 1, sc in next dc] across, tr in next ch-2 corner before first dc in made in same sp, [sc in next dc, tr between next 2 dc in same sp] twice, sc in next dc, tr in same ch-2 sp after last dc made in same sp, sc in next dc on side, rep from * around, join in beg sc. Fasten off.
Rnd 4: Join sky blue with sc in tr after joining of last rnd, *[**fpdc** (see Stitch Guide) around dc on 2nd rnd below, sc in next tr] across, ending with sc in 2nd tr in next corner ch-2 sp, fpdc around next dc, sc in sc in back, fpdc around same dc (corner made), *sc in next tr, fpdc around next dc of rnd 2 below, rep from * across to last tr before next corner ch-2 sp, sc in tr, fpdc around next dc, sc in sc in back, fpdc around same dc (corner made), **fpdc around dc on 2nd rnd below, sc in next tr, rep from ** across, ending with sc in 2nd tr in next corner ch-2 sp, fpdc around next dc, sc in sc in back, fpdc around same dc (corner made), ***sc in next

tr, fpdc around next dc of rnd 2 below, rep from *** across to last tr before next corner ch-2 sp, sc in tr, fpdc around next dc, sc in sc in back, fpdc around same dc *(corner made)*, sc in next tr, fpdc around next dc of rnd 2 below, join in beg sc. Fasten off.

Rnd 5: Join new mint with sc in first fpdc of any corner, 3 sc in next sc *(corner made)*, sc in next fpdc, *[fpdc around next tr, sc in next fpdc] across to last tr before next corner, fpdc around last tr, sc in next fpdc, 3 sc in next sc *(corner made)*, sc in next fpdc, rep from * twice, [fpdc around next tr, sc in next fpdc] across to beg sc, join in beg sc. Fasten off.

Edging

Rnd 1: Join white with sc in same st as joining, sc in next st, 3 sc in next sc *(corner made)*, working across side, work 112 sc evenly sp to 2nd sc of next 3-sc corner, 3 sc in 2nd sc *(corner made)*, working across next side, work 147 sc evenly sp across to 2nd sc of next 3-sc corner, 3 sc in 2nd sc *(corner made)*, working across next side, work 112 sc evenly sp to 2nd sc of next corner, 3 sc in 2nd sc *(corner made)*, working across next side, work 145 sc evenly spaced across to beg sc, join in beg sc. *(530 sc)*

Rnd 2: Sl st in next 3 sc, **beg shell** *(see Special Stitches)* in same sp, *sk next 4 sc, (dc, ch 1) 3 times in next sc, dc in same sc, rep from * 21 times, sk next 4 sc, **shell** *(see Special Stitches)* in next sc, **sk next 4 sc, (dc, ch 1) 3 times in next sc, dc in same sc, rep from ** 28 times, sk next 4 sc, shell in next sc, ***sk next 4 sc, (dc, ch 1) 3 times in next sc, dc in same sc, rep from *** 21 times, sk next 4 sc, shell in next sc, ****sk next 4 sc, (dc, ch 1) 3 times in next sc, dc in same sc, rep from **** 28 times, sk next 4 sc, join in 3rd ch of beg ch-4.

Rnd 3: Ch 1, bpsc around same beg ch, [ch 2, bpsc around next dc] 5 times, *[bpsc around next dc, ch 2] 3 times, bpsc around in dc, rep from * 21 times, [bpsc around next dc, ch 2] 4 times, bpsc around in dc, **[bpsc around next dc, ch 2] 3 times, bpsc around in dc, rep from ** 28 times, [bpsc around next dc, ch 2] 4 times, bpsc around in dc, ***[bpsc around next dc, ch 2] 3 times, bpsc around in dc, rep from *** 21 times, [bpsc around next dc, ch 2] 4 times, bpsc around in dc, ****[bpsc around next dc, ch 2] 3 times, bpsc around in dc, rep from **** 28 times, join in beg bpsc.

Rnd 4: Sl st in next ch-2 sp, ch 1, sc in same sp, [**picot shell** *(see Special Stitches)* in next ch-2 sp, sc in next ch-2 sp] twice, *sc in next ch-2 sp, picot shell in next ch-2 sp, sc in next ch-2 sp, rep from * 21 times, sc in next ch-2 sp, [picot shell in next ch-2 sp, sc in next ch-2 sp] twice, **sc in next ch-2 sp, picot shell in next ch-2 sp, sc in next ch-2 sp, rep from ** 28 times, sc in next ch-2 sp, [picot shell in next ch-2 sp, sc in next ch-2 sp] twice, ***sc in next ch-2 sp, picot shell in next ch-2 sp, sc in next ch-2 sp, rep from *** 21 times, sc in next ch-2 sp, [picot shell in next ch-2 sp, sc in next ch-2 sp] twice, ****sc in next ch-2 sp, picot shell in next ch-2 sp, sc in next ch-2 sp, rep from **** 28 times, join in beg sc. Fasten off. ●

American School of Needlework®
excellence in instruction

TOLL-FREE ORDER LINE or to request a free catalog (800) 582-6643
Customer Service (800) 282-6643, **Fax** (800) 882-6643
Visit DRGnetwork.com.

We have made every effort to ensure the accuracy and completeness of these instructions.
We cannot, however, be responsible for human error, typographical mistakes or variations in individual work.

ISBN: 978-1-59012-216-7   All rights reserved.   Printed in USA   2 3 4 5 6 7 8 9

General Information

Standard Yarn Weight System
Categories of yarn, gauge ranges, and recommended hook sizes

Yarn Weight Symbol & Category Names	SUPER FINE	FINE	LIGHT	MEDIUM	BULKY	SUPER BULKY
Type of Yarns in Category	Sock, Fingering, Baby	Sport, Baby	DK, Light Worsted	Worsted, Afghan, Aran	Chunky, Craft, Rug	Bulky, Roving
Crochet Gauge* Ranges in Single Crochet to 4 inch	21–32 sts	16–20 sts	12–17 sts	11–14 sts	8–11 sts	5–9 sts
Recommended Hook in Metric Size Range	2.25–3.25mm	3.5–4.5mm	4.5–5.5mm	5.5–6.5mm	6.5–9mm	9mm and larger
Recommended Hook U.S. Size Range	B/1–E/4	E/4–7	7–I/9	I/9–K/10½	K/10½–M/13	M/13 and larger

*** GUIDELINES ONLY:** The above reflect the most commonly used gauges and hook sizes for specific yarn categories.

Skill Levels

BEGINNER
Beginner projects for first-time crocheters using basic stitches. Minimal shaping.

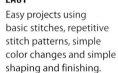

EASY
Easy projects using basic stitches, repetitive stitch patterns, simple color changes and simple shaping and finishing.

INTERMEDIATE
Intermediate projects with a variety of stitches, mid-level shaping and finishing.

EXPERIENCED
Experienced projects using advanced techniques and stitches, detailed shaping and refined finishing.

How to Check Gauge

A correct stitch-gauge is very important. Please take the time to work a stitch-gauge swatch about 4 x 4 inches. Measure the swatch. If the number of stitches and rows is fewer than indicated under "Gauge" in the pattern, your hook is too large. Try another swatch with a smaller size hook. If the number of stitches and rows is more than indicated under "Gauge" in the pattern, your hook is too small. Try another swatch with a larger size hook.

Symbols

* An asterisk (or double asterisk **) is used to mark the beginning of a portion of instructions to be worked more than once; thus, "rep from * twice more" means after working the instructions once, repeat the instructions following the asterisk twice more (3 times in all).

[] Brackets are used to enclose instructions that should be worked the exact number of times specified immediately following the brackets, such as "[2 sc in next dc, sc in next dc] twice."

[] Brackets and () parentheses are used to provide additional information to clarify instructions.

Stitch Guide

For more complete information, visit **AnniesAttic.com**

Abbreviations

beg	begin/beginning
bpdc	back post double crochet
bpsc	back post single crochet
bptr	back post treble crochet
CC	contrasting color
ch	chain stitch
ch-	refers to chain or space previously made (i.e., ch-1 space)
ch sp	chain space
cl	cluster
cm	centimeter(s)
dc	double crochet
dec	decrease/decreases/decreasing
dtr	double treble crochet
fpdc	front post double crochet
fpsc	front post single crochet
fptr	front post treble crochet
g	gram(s)
hdc	half double crochet
inc	increase/increases/increasing
lp(s)	loop(s)
MC	main color
mm	millimeter(s)
oz	ounce(s)
pc	popcorn
rem	remain/remaining
rep	repeat(s)
rnd(s)	round(s)
RS	right side
sc	single crochet
sk	skip(ped)
sl st	slip stitch
sp(s)	space(s)
st(s)	stitch(es)
tog	together
tr	treble crochet
trtr	triple treble crochet
WS	wrong side
yd(s)	yard(s)
yo	yarn over

Chain—ch: Yo, pull through lp on hook.

Slip stitch—sl st: Insert hook in st, pull through both lps on hook.

Single crochet—sc: Insert hook in st, yo, pull through st, yo, pull through both lps on hook.

Front post stitch—fp: Back post stitch—bp: When working post st, insert hook from right to left around post st on previous row.

Back   Front

Front loop—front lp Back loop— back lp

Front Loop   Back Loop

Half double crochet—hdc: Yo, insert hook in st, yo, pull through st, yo, pull through all 3 lps on hook.

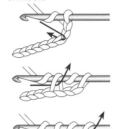

Double crochet—dc: Yo, insert hook in st, yo, pull through st, [yo, pull through 2 lps] twice.

Change colors: Drop first color; with 2nd color, pull through last 2 lps of st.

Treble crochet—tr: Yo twice, insert hook in st, yo, pull through st, [yo, pull through 2 lps] 3 times.

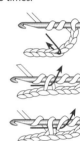

Double treble crochet—dtr: Yo 3 times, insert hook in st, yo, pull through st, [yo, pull through 2 lps], 4 times.

Single crochet decrease (sc dec): (Insert hook, yo, draw lp through) in each of the sts indicated, yo, draw through all lps on hook.

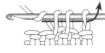

Example of 2-sc dec

Half double crochet decrease (hdc dec): (Yo, insert hook, yo, draw lp through) in each of the sts indicated, yo, draw through all lps on hook.

Example of 2-hdc dec

Double crochet decrease (dc dec): (Yo, insert hook, yo, draw loop through, draw through 2 lps on hook) in each of the sts indicated, yo, draw through all lps on hook.

Example of 2-dc dec

Treble crochet decrease (tr dec): Holding back last lp of each st, tr in each of the sts indicated, yo, pull through all lps on hook.

US		UK
sl st (slip stitch)	=	sc (single crochet)
sc (single crochet)	=	dc (double crochet)
hdc (half double crochet)	=	htr (half treble crochet)
dc (double crochet)	=	tr (treble crochet)
tr (treble crochet)	=	dtr (double treble crochet)
dtr (double treble crochet)	=	ttr (triple treble crochet)
skip	=	miss